The Opossum at Night

A Division of The McGraw·Hill Companies

Columbus, Ohio

www.sra4kids.com

SRA/McGraw-Hill

A Division of The **McGraw·Hill** *Companies*

Send all inquiries to:
SRA/McGraw-Hill
8787 Orion Place
Columbus, OH 43240-4027

ISBN 0-07-569758-0
 2 3 4 5 6 7 8 9 DBH 05 04 03 02

The opossum does not like the light.
It is too bright. She sees better at night.

When it is night, she wakes.
She hunts for insects to feed her babies.

A dog frightens the opossum.
The opossum freezes. She stays still
and plays dead.
She "plays opossum."

Night is over. It begins to get light.

The opossum returns to her tree.
Her babies are waiting.

"It is time for sleep," she tells her babies.
"We might play again tonight."